America's
Christian Heritage

ISBN   Paperback: 979-8-9924813-2-7
ISBN   eBook: 979-8-9924813-3-4

Library of Congress Control Number: 2025913009

Published By:

Publisher Provider:

America's
Christian Heritage

Pastor John H. Miller

BOOKMARC
ALLIANCE

TABLE OF CONTENTS

PREFACE

In June 2007, President Obama told CBS, "Whatever we once were, we are no longer a Christian nation — at least, not just. We are also a Jewish nation, a Muslim nation, a Buddhist nation, and a Hindu nation, and a nation of nonbelievers."…In 2009, he said we "do not consider ourselves a Christian nation" at all.[1] I think many of us would agree that our laws and culture are becoming not just non-Christian but anti-Christian, i.e., anti-Bible and anti-Jesus Christ. We have thrown away the Christian heritage of our Founders. So, what has our new direction given us? Out of control crime, destruction of the traditional family, out of control debt, the 'sacrament' of abortion, teens graduating high school who can't read, a sexual free-for-all, pedophilia, euthanasia, an illegal drug crisis, violence, corruption everywhere, loss of national pride, historical revisionism, increasing government control over every area of life, etc. It's almost like we have lost our national soul. When President Obama said, "we do not consider ourselves a Christian nation", he was probably unaware he addressed the root of America's decline, we've abandoned the God our Founders cherished.

This booklet is intended to be a brief historical overview of the Christian heritage of America. It is undeniable that America was once a Christian nation. Hopefully we will see the error of our ways and turn back to our Judeo-Christian heritage.

America's
Christian Heritage

When we celebrate the 4th of July as Independence Day, we pause to remember that our Founding Fathers gave us a nation built on God and the Bible. This historic day marks the adoption of the Declaration of Independence by the Continental Congress declaring that the thirteen American colonies now regarded themselves as a new nation, a *"United States of America."* As such we were officially no longer part of the British Empire.

Think of the Declaration of Independence as our National Birth Certificate. Born out of Biblical principles and the foundation of freedom, to this very day we remain the longest ongoing Constitutional Republic in the history of the world. But blessings such as these do not happen by chance or accident. Nor are they merely the inventions of men. On the contrary, they are blessings of God Almighty. The Psalmist echoed this truth when he wrote,

"Blessed is the nation whose God is the Lord, the people whom he has chosen as his heritage!" - Psalm 33:12 (ESV)

Today, however, there is a lot of confusion concerning America's Christian roots. In this booklet, we'll explore America's godly heritage and the Christian faith of our Founders. If you're a Christian, you'll discover more about your own dual citizenship as a believer in Christ, and you'll be challenged to be a voice in society for the Christian principles that made our nation great. If you're not a Christian, I hope you'll consider the sources for my premise and realize the Biblical and Christian influence most of our Founders embraced. There's also a section at the end of this booklet written just for you. It will show you how to experience the wonderful love of our Savior, Jesus Christ.

America's Christian Roots

OUR FOUNDERS VIEW OF THE BIBLE AND JESUS CHRIST

Consider the heartfelt convictions of those who were instrumental in America's inception.

President Andrew Johnson wrote, *"The Bible is the Rock on which our Republic rests."*[2]

Benjamin Rush, signer of the Declaration of Independence and was instrumental in the founding of public schools, stated,*"The great enemy of the salvation of man never invented a more effective means of eliminating Christianity from the world than by persuading mankind that it was improper to read the Bible at schools."*[3]

John Quincy Adams, our sixth President, wrote, *"No book in the world deserves to be so unceasingly studied and so profoundly meditated upon as the Bible."*[4]

John Jay, the first Chief Justice of the Supreme Court, wrote,*"The Bible is the best of all books, for it is the Word of God and teaches us how to be happy in this world and the next."*[5]

In 1781, Robert Aitken, the official printer of the Continental Congress, asked Congress for permission to print Bibles for use in schools. The full Congress approved his request and printed in the front of each a Congressional endorsement stating, *"Resolved that the United States in Congress recommend this Bible to the inhabitants of the United States."*[6]

Can you imagine Congress agreeing to this today?

In 1982, *Newsweek* reported, *"Historians are discovering that the Bible, perhaps even more than the Constitution, is our founding document."*[7]

That is a secular publication—but it was also written forty years ago.

Samuel Adams, signer of the Declaration, declared, *"I rely on the merits of Jesus Christ for a pardon of all my sins."*[8]

John Witherspoon, another signer, said, *"Jesus Christ is the only savior of sinners; if you are not reconciled to God through Jesus Christ, you must forever perish."*[9]

This is only a sample of our Founders views. Clearly, the majority of the Founding Fathers were God-fearing men, many of whom possessed a deep faith in the Lord Jesus Christ and the Bible.

God and the American Revolution

Do you remember these words from the Declaration of Independence? On July 4,1776, our country's founders declared, *"We hold these truths to be self-evident, that all men are created equal, that they are endowed by their Creator with certain unalienable Rights, that among these are Life, Liberty and the pursuit of Happiness."*[10]

These were not mere opinions blurted around drinks at the local men's club, but rather truths that are "self-evident" (obvious) to everyone. And where do these truths (or basic human rights) come from? Kings? Governments? A voting booth? No, they are sovereignly endowed by the Creator, the same Creator every signer of that Declaration recognized as God.

Consider Ben Franklin, who clearly believed in God, but some believe was not a professing Christian. Franklin motioned at the Constitutional Convention in September 1787: *"…groping as it were in the dark to find political truth… how has it happened, Sir, that we have not hitherto once thought of humbly applying to the Father of lights to illuminate our understandings? In the beginning of the Contest with Great Britain…we had daily prayer… for the divine protection. Our prayers…were graciously answered."*[11]

And Franklin was not alone but merely stated an obvious reality. In fact, the Christian emphasis manifested so often by the Americans during the Revolution caused one British governor to write to Great Britain complaining that, *"If you ask an American who is his master, he'll tell you he has none. And he has no governor but Jesus Christ."* [12]

Again, from President John Quincy Adams, *"The highest glory of the American Revolution was this: it connected, in one indissoluble bond, the principles of civil government with the principles of Christianity."* [13]

Our Bill of Rights gives every individual the right to practice their religion or the right to reject religion. And the Framers of our Constututution did not force people to become Christians, but instead helped create a free country, giving all Americans the assurance there would be no state church like the church of England, which persecuted genuine believers in Jesus Christ.

Even so, Christianity was nevertheless encoded into America's conception. It's in our national "DNA." So much so that if you were elected to Congress in the State of Delaware in 1776, this is what you agreed to: *"Every person who shall be a chosen member of either House, or appointed to any office or place of trust shall make and subscribe the following declaration, 'I_____ do profess faith in God the Father, and in Jesus Christ His only Son, and the Holy Ghost, one God- blessed forevermore; and I do acknowledge the Holy Scriptures and the Old and New Testament to be given by divine inspiration."* [14] Requiring such an oath today in Delaware, or in any State today, would immediately ignite a national outrage.

Christianity and Early Education in America

Dr. Lawrence A. Cremin, who holds a Ph.D. from Columbia University, has said that during the Colonial Period the Bible was *"the single most important cultural influence in the lives of Anglo-Americans."*[15] To illustrate this claim, The New England Primer used to teach children of the Colonies how to read and understand the ABC's using stories from the Bible.[16]

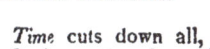

Time cuts down all,
Both great and small.

Uriah's beauteous wife
Made David seek his life.

Whales in the sea,
God's voice obey.

Xerxes the great did die,
And so must you and I.

Youth forward slips—
Death soonest nips.

Zac-che-us, he
Did climb the tree,
Our Lord to see.

in the branches of an Oak tree in Boscobel wood, where he saw his enemies in full pursuit of him. This Oak tree was regarded, by the friends of the King, with much veneration, after having afforded shelter to the Royal Fugitive.

In *Adam's* fall,
We sinned all.

Heaven to find,
The *Bible* mind.

The *Cat* doth play,
And after slay.

The *Dog* will bite
A thief at night.

An *Eagle's* flight
Is out of sight.

The idle *Fool*
Is whipt at school.

1777 edition:

The letter A: "In Adams fall, we sinned all."

The letter B: "Heaven to find, the Bible mind."

The letter C: "Christ crucify'd.", and so on.

By the time Colonial children learned their A, B, C's, they were also well acquainted with Bible stories and biblical concepts of right and wrong. But within two centuries, schools had switched to readers like "Dick and Jane" books, which embraced cultural, Biblical concepts but no longer taught the historical accounts from the Bible.

Worse, now schools use books like *"Heather Has 2 Mommies"*, *normalizing homosexual marriage.*[17] Is it any wonder why test scores have dropped, along with the overall moral decline of our youth and a rising crime rate? One of the main reasons why they abandoned the New England Primer was due to a growing number of non-Christian families who did not want their children exposed to the Bible. Secular educators also pushed to remove all Christian education from the public schools, including the removal of the Ten Commandments from schools. It's outrageous that we don't want America's children to be told it's wrong to lie, steal and kill! The ACLU brought numerous lawsuits against Christianity being taught in any form in the public schools. In other words, our public education system wanted God, and everything associated with Him to be removed from the minds of children.

Ironically, what is amazing to consider, is the number of our country's major colleges and universities that were founded by Christians and built upon Christian principles. In fact, 106 of the first 108 colleges in America were founded upon biblical principles and mandates. Consider the Christian heritage of Harvard: In the 2nd

Rules and Precepts of that once respected institution, it was stated: (2) Let every student be plainly instructed…the main end of his life and studies is, to know God and Jesus Christ which is eternal life… the only foundation of all sound knowledge and learning…[18]

Fast forward to May 2016, when the Washington Times reported that a Harvard law professor, Mark Tushnet, called for liberals to begin treating like Nazis those who subscribe to Christian or conservative beliefs.[19] You read that right. *Nazis.* In just a few hundred years, Harvard went from "*The Scripture defines and guides us*" to "*all Christians are Nazis.*" Sadly, what was once considered as *holy* is now seen by many as *Hitler-esque*. The words of Isaiah the prophet come to mind, **"woe to those who call evil good and good evil, who put darkness for light and light for darkness." Isaiah 5:20 (ESV).** We would do well to heed the advice of Dr. Benjamin Rush, a signer of the Declaration of Independence and significant influencer of public schools, who wrote, The Bible… should be read in our schools in preference to all other books because it contains the greatest portion of that kind of knowledge which is calculated to produce private and public happiness.[20]

AMERICA'S NATIONAL MOTTO, "IN GOD WE TRUST"

Have you ever noticed that little phrase on our currency? The roots of our national motto, *"In God We Trust,"* actually comes from our National Anthem, *"The Star-Spangled Banner,"* written by Francis Scott Key in 1814.[21] After witnessing the bombardment of Fort McHenry by British ships in the War of 1812, Key was inspired by the large American flag, the Star-Spangled Banner, flying triumphantly above the Fort during the American victory. In Verse 4, he declares, *"Praise the Power that hath made and preserved us a nation!... Then conquer we must, when our cause it is just...And this be our motto: 'In God is our trust'..."*

"In God We Trust" first appeared on U.S. coins in 1864 and has appeared on our paper currency since 1957. It then became our National Motto, adopted in 1956 by Congress to differentiate the United States of America from atheistic communism.[22] Two years earlier, Congress had added the words *"under God"* to the Pledge of Allegiance. That was just a generation ago.

It is evident that over the lifetime of our nation, a spiritual darkness has descended, gaining in both the past and present a foothold in American culture.

AMERICA: THE STAIN OF HER PAST

Though we unequivocally and totally reject the institution and practice of slavery in any culture, modern historical revisionists are wrong about the narrative of slavery in America.

The Founding Fathers and Slavery – WallBuilders.[23]

1. Slavery was not introduced in America by the Founding Fathers but rather by Spain 200 years earlier. Prior to that, Indian tribes made slaves of their enemies. The Revolutionary War was the turning point to rid our country of slavery. Many of the Founders complained that Great Britain forcefully imposed the vile of slavery upon the Colonies. Thomas Jefferson said, *"King George III has waged cruel war against human nature itself, violating its most sacred rights of life and liberty of a distant people... carrying them into slavery in another hemisphere."*[23] Benjamin Franklin, in a 1773 letter to Dean Woodward, confirmed that whenever the Americans had attempted to end slavery, the British government had indeed thwarted those attempts.

2. From John Quincy Adams, our 6th President, *"The inconsistency of slavery with the principles of the Declaration of Independence was lamented by all the southern patriots of the Revolution. Never from their lips was heard one syllable*

of attempt to justify the institution of slavery. They saw that before the principles of the Declaration of Independence, slavery was destined sooner or later to be banished from the earth."[23]

3. Consider the Christian roots of the abolitionist movement. African American, and Stanford economist, Thomas Sowell writes, *"While slavery was common to all civilizations, only one civilization developed a moral revulsion against it.... Moreover, within Western civilization, the principle impetus for the abolition of slavery came first from very conservative religious activists – people who would today be called 'the religious right.'...This story is not 'politically correct' in today's terms. Hence it is ignored, as if it never happened."* [24]

4. Many of the Founders never owned slaves. John Adams, our 2nd President, *"[M]y opinion against it [slavery] has always been known . . . [N]ever in my life did I own a slave."* [23] Admittedly, some Founders did own slaves but released them when America separated from Great Britain, (e.g., George Washington). Though he was initially wrong, does that negate the sacrifices he made to give us freedom? Likewise, we're grateful for the efforts of Martin Luther King, who was a voice for freedom, though some documents from the era suggest his personal moral character was less than admirable. We don't cast away great leaders, past or present because of their sin. We are all flawed humans. We all make mistakes; our Founders weren't perfect either. Yet God nevertheless used them to create the greatest bastion of freedom in world history. Slavery and racism are wrong, but they are not unpardonable sins. Otherwise, God would have never redeemed a former slave captain, John Newton, who repented, became a Christian, and wrote, *"Amazing Grace"*.[25]

Let me unequivocally repeat for emphasis, that the slavery of our past along with present human slavery and trafficking (40 million worldwide), is wrong, sinful, and inexcusable. But it is a mistake to cite past sins like this as justification for casting away freedom and the Constitution and replace them with godless socialism or communism.

RACE AND EQUALITY: THE BIBLE, THE FOUNDERS AND MODERN CULTURE

The Biblical starting place for a discussion of race and equality begins in **Genesis 1:26, "Then God said, 'Let us make man in our image, after our likeness." (ESV).** We can trace every race and ethnicity on the planet throughout history to two people. We all have the same parents and ancestors. We are all *one human race.* In the New Testament, we read, **"And he made from one man (Adam) every nation of mankind to live on all the face of the earth… Acts 17:26 (ESV).**

So again, in a foundational sense, we aren't African, American, Caucasian, Hispanic or Asian, (i.e., many races), but rather one race, the human race, all created by God. **"And in the church, there is no longer Jew or Gentile, slave or free, male and female. For you are all one in Christ Jesus." Gal. 3:28 (NLT).** Therefore, Jesus, not the state, is the great equalizer and unifier of the races. Remember, the Founders' view of race and equality: We hold these truths to be self-evident, that all men are created equal.[10] So why weren't all equal? Two reasons stand out.(1) Man's inherent sinfulness, greed and self-righteousness, and (2) Philosophies and ideologies promoted by systems of government.

One growing cultural view of race and equality is embodied in a Marxist ideology called, *"Critical Race Theory,"*[36] a political philosophy that views society as oppressors and the oppressed as victims. They claim the government's role is to make us all *"equal"*. *"Social justice warriors"* are then the agents of change. To be 'woke' means you're onboard with the revolution.

However, their goal is not equal opportunity under law, but rather guaranteed equal outcomes forced upon us by the state. They claim that socialism and communism are preferable to individual freedom, while conveniently ignoring failed socialist nations like Venezuela and Cuba. They also ignore that in the last century 100 million citizens were murdered in communist states like China. These social justice proponents aren't interested in helping us forgive one another for the mistakes of the past. Instead, they want to replace the Constitution and fundamentally change America into a state more resembling the tyrannical governments of nations like Russia or China.

We must fight these ideologies with the same moral passion that once freed us from England's rule that birthed our Revolution. This push for a one-world, all-powerful government is from an antichrist spirit that will one day give birth to the Biblically named Anti-Christ.

ABORTION, THE BIBLE, AND THE DECLARATION OF INDEPENDENCE

In light of Supreme Court or legislative decisions on abortion, we, as Bible-believing Christians, appeal to Scripture. When does the Bible say human life begins? Or when does a baby in the womb actually become a person? **"You (God) made all the delicate, inner parts of my body and knit me together in my mother's womb...15 You watched me as...I was woven together in the dark of the womb. You saw me before I was born..." Psalm 139:13–16 (NLT) "I knew you before I formed you in your mother's womb. Before you were born I set you apart and appointed you as my prophet to the nations." Jeremiah 1:5 (NLT)** When Elizabeth heard Mary's greeting, **"the unborn baby inside her...... jumped with joy."** Luke 1:41–44 (NCV)

So, it's clear that the Bible teaches human life begins in the womb, and furthermore, science confirms it. *The American College of Pediatricians:* states the predominance of human biological research confirms that human life begins at conception—fertilization.[39]

Scientists at Northwestern University Just Captured The Flash of Light That Sparks When a Sperm Meets an Egg.[26]

So why then is abortion Biblically wrong? Simple. God declared, **"You shall not murder." Exodus 20:13 (ESV)** Murder is defined as the intentional, premeditated, and unlawful taking of human life. Murder usurps the authority that belongs to God as to who lives, who dies, and when they die.

For me, the starting place for a discussion about abortion is simple: God tells us in His Word that human life begins in the womb, and He forbids the murder of innocent life. Period. If we respect God's Word, our opinion about abortion will be shaped by the Bible, along with our commitment to marriage and our sexual practices that produce babies. There would be an exponential change in abortion rates if we just lived by God's standards for sex and marriage. Courts and legislatures may pass laws, but our love and fear of God should determine what we believe and do. Dred Scott was wrong about slavery, and it was overturned because of a basic commitment to biblical morality and human rights, and so was Roe v Wade about abortion.

The Declaration of Independence agrees with this conviction. We hold these truths to be self-evident, that **all men are created equal,** that they are **endowed by their Creator with certain unalienable rights, that among these are Life,** Liberty and the pursuit of Happiness.--*That to secure these rights, Governments are instituted among Men, deriving their just powers from the consent of the governed,*"[10]

1. The Supreme Court recognized that the right to make laws about abortion belongs to the states so "we the People" could decide. It's called Federalism, i.e., divided political power between states and the federal government. Citizens vote for people to represent them. But Communism takes away the people's voice and puts all power in the hands of a centralized government. This is what we must fight against.

2. As previously cited, it was this Biblical principle 'all men are created equal' that overturned the evil of slavery.

3. Not only did our Declaration of Independence ultimately do away with slavery, it protects the right for life for all Americans, including those in the womb. Our 1st unalienable right, the right to life, is a right given by God, not government.

Bible believing Christians aren't just against abortion, but we're also involved in helping moms and kids in a big way. At the church I pastor, we own a facility called 'Grace House', a 10-bedroom facility to help pregnant moms and moms who have kids who are homeless and in great need. Grace House, was started by a woman named Karen (a former homeless mom) and Artie Rayfield, helps young moms in crisis transition to a life of stability. We also support both Crisis Pregnancy Centers in town and all foster care ministries in the area.

GENDER AND SEXUALITY

The current lie of gender choice elevates politics over science and is indelibly marking and ruining a generation of young people. A biology professor at a Texas community college has claimed he was fired after teaching a lesson about how sex is determined by X and Y chromosomes.[27] The so-called Pride Month ended in NYC several years ago with the chant "we're queer, we're here, we're coming for your children."[37] And don't think this is not happening. Third graders in a Connecticut school were shown a video about gender identity without parental consent.[28] As a pastor, I've personally wrestled during pride month with how some Christians and churches address this issue. Somehow we must be able to show genuine Christian love while unashamedly proclaiming Biblical truth. After all, people's eternal souls are at stake. I believe, **"There's room at the cross for you."** And that includes all of us. However, when churches sponsor, *"drag queen story hour"* they've crossed the line of God- honoring sexual behavior. I believe surface solutions and even laws are not the ultimate solution. We believe that every human being is valuable to God, and that the root problem of all sin can only be changed by a personal encounter with Jesus Christ.

THE BREAKDOWN OF THE TRADITIONAL FAMILY

Today, 1 in 4 kids live in a home without a dad. Most single moms struggle to survive. And as government incentivises single motherhood (bearing children out of wedlock) it oversteps its authority and attempts to take the place of God. The result is that we have less freedom. Thomas Paine, Founding Father said, *"That government is best which governs least."*[30] More government overreach and societal deterioration is evidenced by the following:

- New York City now wants to ban wood-fired pizza to "save the environment."

- Cities defund the police, whose Biblical role is to restrain evil.

- We're rewriting history and tearing down statues much like Chairman Mao did in Communist China.

- We're spiraling downward in out-of-control debt.

- We're moving backwards in race relations. MLK taught us to judge people by their character not skin color, yet we deal with past discrimination by discriminating against people based on the color of their skin.

- Drug epidemics and violence are an accepted way of life on our streets.

- Pornography is one of the biggest industries on the internet, bringing in billions each year.

Yes, something has happened in America in the last 60 years. In the 1960's, the Supreme Court removed the 10 commandments and Bible reading from schools and manger scenes from public buildings. Now religious freedom, (i.e., the right to live out your faith as you see fit) is itself under attack. There is open hostility to Christianity in America and Christians are now being marginalized and bullied. Christian bakers and florists have had to consider violating their biblical convictions or be fined. Believers are fired for privately standing for traditional marriage. Crosses are forcibly removed from cemeteries. Chaplains are told not to pray in Jesus name, and "under God" is often deleted the Pledge of Allegiance.

So what happened to our country? In 1991, George Barna found that 86% of U.S. adults held a biblical view of God. In 2021, it dropped to 46%.[31] What about belief in the Bible as *"the accurate Word of God"?* it was 70% in 1991 but is now 41%. What about Americans who believe they'll go to heaven because they accept Jesus as their personal Savior? 36% in 1991. 30% now. The percentage of those who don't believe, or know, if God exists? 12% in 2011 to 34% in 2021. 43% of Millennials are now apart of this demographic, labelled the "Don'ts".

So, what's the solution? A lesson from ancient Israel would serve us well. The prophet Jeremiah wrote, **"Are they ashamed of their disgusting actions? Not at all"**—they don't even know how to blush!... This is what the Lord says: **"Stop at the crossroads and look around. Ask for the old, godly way, and walk in it. Travel its path, and you will find rest for your souls..."**] **[Jeremiah 6:15-16 (NLT)**. The Bible calls this *repentance* or returning to God. When individuals turn to God and His ways, the result is a personal spiritual awakening and oftentimes a national spiritual awakening.

THE ASSAULT ON RELIGIOUS FREEDOM IN AMERICA

In the Rotunda of the US Congress,[32] there hangs a series of paintings reflecting America's Christian heritage. There, we see the baptism of Pocahontas, who was the first convert to Christianity in Virginia. We see a painting of the Pilgrims leaving Holland, praying around the Geneva Bible. There is Desoto crossing the Mississippi River, planting a cross and dedicating the land to God. And when Columbus landed on the Florida coast, he did the same, planting a cross in the sand and dedicating the land to God. However imperfect past explorers and founders may have been, at their core was a desire to serve the Creator-God.

However, something has happened in America in the last 60 years. As mentioned before, religious freedom (i.e. the right to live out your faith as you see fit) is now under attack. Today, we are witnessing an open hostility to Christianity in America. Christians are being bullied, "*cancelled*," told to be quiet, vilified in social media, and become the objects of lawsuits and other acts of hostility. This soft persecution began in the 1960's with the Supreme Court's removal of Judeo-Christian morals and practices from schools, along with manger scenes from public buildings. Since then, judges sought to restrict prayer in schools. Christians have been fired for standing up and defending traditional marriage. And even simply declaring that a man is a man and can never be a woman can draw the worst kind of hatred and attacks from culture.

Thankfully, freedom of religion is experiencing a comeback in the courts. According to Kelly Shackleford of First Liberty Institute, we're starting to win as newly appointed judges are upholding the Constitution.[33] In President Trump's first term (regardless of whether you like or hate him), 132 federal judges were confirmed who ostensibly believe in applying the Constitution today. In other words, they still believe in America as she was originally designed and conceived.

But as far back as the 1960's and even earlier, secular humanists began attempting to destroy every vestige of our Christian heritage, replacing it with a man-centered, godless, government-controlled state. Along with this, they are intent on destroying our First Amendment guarantee of religious freedom as well. As we've learned, originally when our nation was founded, the majority of the men who gave birth to the greatest nation on earth had a sincere belief in God and the Bible. Again, this is not to say that they were all practicing Christians, but rather that the vast majority held to a basic belief in the Creator and in a Judeo-Christian morality as found in the Bible. They also believed that a God-given freedom, along with Biblical principles, were the only way to build and preserve a civil and prosperous society.

Tragically, this belief is not widely taught or recognized in America today. Instead, our Founders are now depicted as greedy, privileged white men who only gave lip service to God and only came to America to pillage and enslave people for their own gain. This is gross misrepresentation. Admittedly, they weren't perfect. However, together they nevertheless left an indelible mark of Christianity in their writings, documents, and through the monuments they erected and inspired.

I believe they would be shocked, appalled, offended, and deeply saddened at what their United States of America has become.

WHAT CAN WE DO TO COUNTER RELIGIOUS HOSTILITY?

Is there anything we can do to help turn the tide, and see America return to God and Christian persecution and discrimination cease? I believe so. Here are a few principles to guide us as we move forward in these challenging days:

1. Be Like Paul

   We can use our rights to get involved. Stand up for your rights as an American citizen. Know your constitutional rights and fight for religious freedom. Paul himself appealed to his Roman citizenship to avoid unlawful persecution. In Acts 22, when they had stretched him out for the whips, Paul said, **"Is it lawful for you to flog a man who is a Roman citizen and uncondemned?" Acts 22:25 (ESV)**. Our Bill of Rights states, (1) *Congress shall make no law respecting an establishment of religion or **prohibiting the free exercise thereof***"

In other words, this guarantees our freedom to live out our Christian faith in a free society. And even though it's in the Bill of Rights, we still sometimes have to fight for it. You may recall the story of Jake Phillips, and his Masterpiece Cake Shop in Colorado.[34] In the biggest religious liberty case of 2018, the US Supreme Court sided 7–2 against a State Commission that unfairly singled out a Christian baker who declined to decorate a cake for a same-sex wedding. Jake had to fight in the court system, and you may one day have to do the same. Be ready.

2. Be Like Daniel
   In spite of what others do, you and I must do what God says is right, even if it's widely unpopular. In Daniel 6, we read of Babylon's governing officials agreeing that "*the king should make a law that will be strictly enforced. Give orders that... any person who prays to anyone...except to you, Your Majesty—will be thrown into the den of lions...*" But when Daniel learned that the law had been signed, he went home and ..."**He prayed three times a day, just as he had always done**"... **Daniel 6:7-10 (NLT)**.

You see, Daniel had already made up his mind beforehand to remain loyal to his God, and no government, king, or culture would ever deter him from obedience to his Lord.

3. Be Like Jonah
   Speak the truth in love in hopes of a spiritual awakening. God told Jonah, "Go to...Nineveh and **proclaim to it the message I give you**."..."*Forty more days and Nineveh will be overthrown.*" *And the result?* "**The Ninevites believed God...**" **Jonah 3:2-5 (NIV)**.

We do not know if there will be a last day's revival in America, but it is our hope. But what we do know is that God has commanded us to be salt and light in a depraved and dark world (Matthew 5:13-16; Philippians 2:15)

Never underestimate the power of God working through a single believer – whether it be Paul, Daniel, Jonah...or <u>you</u>!

CONCLUSION: PRAY FOR AND PROMOTE A SPIRITUAL AWAKENING IN AMERICA

So what makes a *"Christian nation"?* According to Supreme Court Justice Brewer in the late 1800's, *America is* "of all the nations of the world most justly called a Christian nation because Christianity has so largely shaped and molded it."[35] In 1931, the Supreme Court said, *"We are a Christian people…according to one another the equal right of religious freedom and acknowledging with reverence the duty of obedience to the will of God."*[38] That's the America we pray for, long for, and fight for.

By following the examples of Paul, Daniel, and Jonah, you can help promote a spiritual awakening in our country. And by praying, you can directly tap into the Power Source to help make that possible. With that in mind, would you be willing to take a few moments right now and every day and pray for our country?

Perhaps a prayer like the one below expresses the desire of your heart. If so, why not pray it now?

God, I thank you Lord that I was born in America. We are blessed because we have freedoms and rights that originally and ultimately came from You. And I thank you for those things. However, many in our nation have walked away from you, God. Many are lost or there are many who are held captive in sin. They've been deceived by the enemy. So, dear Lord, would You send Your Spirit to sweep across our nation and begin to move in the hearts of all Americans. Would You turn us back to You, Lord, that we would, obey your commandments and follow the Bible. God, we pray that you would turn the hearts of our leaders towards You. Touch our young people that they wouldn't be deceived, but that they would be a generation that pursues you. God, we need a spiritual awakening that turns our hearts to You. Please Lord, have mercy on America, in Jesus name, Amen.

HOW DO I BECOME A CHRISTIAN?

The Bible teaches that, if you choose today to turn to God, believe in Jesus and follow Him you can experience a spiritual rebirth. Your sins will be forgiven; you will begin a personal relationship with God and have the assurance of knowing that you will go to heaven when you die.

HOW TO KNOW JESUS CHRIST AS YOUR PERSONAL SAVIOR

The Bible is the foundation for Christianity and truth. These verses explain God's plan for your salvation:

GOD LOVES YOU

"For God so loved the world, that he gave his only son, that whoever believes in him should not perish but have eternal life. "– John 3:16

"But God shows his love for us in that while we were still sinners, Christ died for us." – Romans 5:8

ALL ARE SINNERS

"For all have sinned and fall short of the glory of God." – Romans 3:23

As it is written: "none is righteous, no, not one" – Romans 3:10

GOD'S REMEDY FOR SIN

"For the wages of sin is death; but the free gift of God is eternal life in Christ Jesus our Lord." – Romans 6:23 "But to all who did receive him, who believed in his name, he gave the right to become children of God." – John 1:12

ALL MAY BE SAVED

"Behold, I stand at the door and knock. If anyone hears my voice and opens the door, I come in to him and eat with him, and he with me." – Revelation 3:20

"For everyone who calls on the name of the Lord will be saved." – Romans 10:13

"But these are written so that you may believe that Jesus is the Christ, the Son of God, and that by believing you may have life in his name." – John 20:31

PRAY

"God, I confess that I am a sinner and I am in need of salvation. I believe Jesus died on the cross for my sins and rose again to bring me new life. I ask You to forgive me and come into my life. Today, I choose to follow You as my Lord and Savior. Amen." (*Used with permission from www.gideons.org)

Sign: _____

Date: _____

ASSURANCE OF YOUR SALVATION

Assurance for the believer comes directly from God's Word. The Gospel tells us that because Christ died for us, anyone who trusts in Him may know that their sins have been forgiven, once and for all.

"Because, if you confess with your mouth that Jesus is Lord and believe in your heart that God raised him from the dead, you will be saved." – Romans 10:9

"Truly, truly, I say to you, whoever hears my word and believes him who sent me has eternal life. He does not come into judgment, but has passed from death to life." – John 5:24

WHAT DO I DO NOW?

1. Read your Bible every day and talk to God in prayer.

2. Become an active part of a Bible-believing local church.

3. Send a text to 97000 and type *"RESTORED"* to receive 10 short videos I recorded to help your spiritual growth.

4. Follow me and watch my daily videos for spiritual encouragement on, "Facebook, Instagram, TikTok,

Lemon8, and Truth Social. Search for Pastor John Miller, Pastor John H Miller, or gardening pastor.

5. Download the Church on the Rock app by searching for COTR TXK. You will find helpful sermons and a daily Bible reading plan.

END NOTES

1. Barack Obama, interview by Harry Smith, *CBS Early Show*, June 2007, quoted in Todd Starnes, *God Less America: Real Stories from the Front Lines of the Attack on Traditional Values* (Lake Mary, FL: FrontLine, 2014), 43.

2. Andrew Jackson, quoted in William J. Federer, *America's God and Country: Encyclopedia of Quotations* (Coppell, TX: FAME Publishing, 1996), 308.

3. Rush to Jeremy Belknap, July 13, 1789, *Letters of Benjamin Rush*, I:521.

4. John Quincy Adams, *Letters of John Quincy Adams to His Son on the Bible and Its Teachings* (Auburn: Derby, Miller and Co., 1848), 61.

5. John Jay, quoted in William J. Federer, *America's God and Country: Encyclopedia of Quotations* (Coppell, TX: FAME Publishing, 1996), 318.

6. United States Continental Congress, *"Resolution of Congress Approving the Aitken Bible,"* September 12, 1782, quoted in Library of Congress, *Religion and the Founding of the American Republic,*

7. Newsweek, *"How the Bible Made America,"* December 27, 1982, 44–52.

8. From the Last Will & Testament of Samuel Adams, attested December 29, 1790; Samuel Adams, *Life & Public Services of Samuel Adams*, ed. William V. Wells (Boston: Little, Brown & Co, 1865), II:379.

9. Witherspoon, *"The Absolute Necessity of Salvation Through Christ,"* January 2, 1758, *Works*, V:278.

10. *The Declaration of Independence*, July 4, 1776, in *The American Declaration of Independence*, National Archives, https://www.archives.gov/founding-docs/declaration-transcript.

11. WallBuilders, *"Franklin's Appeal for Prayer at the Constitutional Convention,"* accessed May 20, 2025, https://wallbuilders.com/resource/franklins-appeal-for-prayer-at-the-constitutional-convention/.

12. Attributed to a British governor during the American Revolution, quoted in William J. Federer, *America's God and Country: Encyclopedia of Quotations* (Coppell, TX: FAME Publishing, 1996), 292.

13. John Quincy Adams, quoted in William J. Federer, *America's God and Country: Encyclopedia of Quotations* (Coppell, TX: FAME Publishing, 1996), 10.

14. Delaware State Constitution of 1776, art. 22, quoted in *The Federal and State Constitutions, Colonial Charters, and Other Organic Laws*, ed. Francis Newton Thorpe, vol. 1 (Washington, DC: Government Printing Office, 1909), 562.

15. Cremin, Lawrence A. *American Education: The Colonial Experience, 1607–1783*. New York: Harper & Row, 1970.

16. *The New England Primer*, 1777 ed. (Boston: Edward Draper, 1777; repr., New York: Arno Press, 1969

17. Newman, Lesléa. *Heather Has Two Mommies*. 2nd ed. Somerville, MA: Candlewick Press, 2015. https://www.penguinrandomhouse.

com/books/249466/heather-has-two-mommies-by-leslea-newman/9780763690427.

18. Christian Heritage Fellowship. "The Christian Founding of Harvard." Accessed May 12, 2025. https://christianheritagefellowship.com/the-christian-founding-of-harvard/.

19. The Washington Times. "Harvard Professor: Start Treating Christians like Nazis." May 10, 2016. https://www.washingtontimes.com/news/2016/may/10/harvard-professor-start-treating-christians-nazis/.

20. Benjamin Rush, "A Defense of the Use of the Bible as a School Book," 1791, quoted in William J. Federer, *America's God and Country: Encyclopedia of Quotations* (Coppell, TX: FAME Publishing, 1996), 562.

21. Francis Scott Key, "The Star-Spangled Banner," 1814, verse 4, *Library of Congress*, accessed May 28, 2025, https://www.loc.gov/item/ihas.200000017/.

22. WallBuilders, "In God We Trust," accessed May 28, 2025, https://wallbuilders.com/in-god-we-trust/.

23. WallBuilders, "The Founding Fathers and Slavery," accessed May 20, 2025, https://wallbuilders.com/resource/the-founding-fathers-and-slavery/.

24. Thomas Sowell, *Black Rednecks and White Liberals* (San Francisco: Encounter Books, 2005), 111.

25. John Newton, *Out of the Depths: The Autobiography of John Newton*, ed. Richard Cecil (Chicago: Moody Publishers, 2003), 87.

26. MacDonald, Fiona. "Scientists at Northwestern University Just Captured the Flash of Light That Sparks When a Sperm Meets an Egg." *Science Alert*, April 26, 2016.

27. Kristine Parks, "Texas Professor Claims He Was Fired for Teaching X and Y Chromosomes Determine Biological Sex," *Fox News*, July 26, 2023.

28. Joshua Q. Nelson, "Connecticut Parents Outraged after School Shows Third Graders Video about Gender Identity without Parental Consent," *Fox News*, May 6, 2022,

29. U.S. Census Bureau, *Living Arrangements of Children Under 18 Years Old: 2022*, Table C3, accessed May 28, 2025, https://www.census.gov/data/tables/2022/demo/families/cps-2022.html.

30. WallBuilders, "Unconfirmed Quotations," accessed May 28, 2025, https://wallbuilders.com/unconfirmed-quotations/.

31. George Barna, *American Worldview Inventory 2021: Release #6 – Biblical Worldview Slips to 6% Among Adults*, Cultural Research Center at Arizona Christian University, May 2021

32. Library of Congress. "Rotunda Paintings in the U.S. Capitol." https://www.aoc.gov/historic-rotunda-paintings.

33. Shackelford, Kelly. *First Liberty Institute Cases*. https://firstliberty.org/.

34. Christianity Today. "Jack Phillips' Masterpiece Cakeshop Wins Supreme Court Free Speech Case." June 2018. https://www.christianitytoday.com/news/2018/june/jack-phillips-masterpiece-cakeshop-wins-supreme-court-free-.html.

35. Brewer, *A Christian Nation* (1905), 57.

36. Imprimus, A Publication of Hillsdale College, March 2021, https://imprimis.hillsdale.edu/wp-content/uploads/2021/04/Imprimis_Mar_3-21_6pgNM.pdf

37. Newsweek, https://www.newsweek.com › video-drag-marchers-chanting-viral-1808870

38. "This Precarious Moment, James Garlow and David Barton. Salem Books, 2018. Page 190"

39. https://acpeds.org/when-human-life-begins/v

BIBLIOGRAPHY

Adams, John Quincy. *Letters of John Quincy Adams to His Son on the Bible and Its Teachings* (Auburn, NY: Derby, Miller & Co., 1848), page 61.

Adams, Samuel. *The Life and Public Services of Samuel Adams.* Edited by William V. Wells. Vol. 2. Boston: Little, Brown & Co., 1865.

Barna, George. *American Worldview Inventory 2021: Release #6 – Biblical Worldview Slips to 6% Among Adults.* Cultural Research Center at Arizona Christian University, May 2021

Brewer, *A Christian Nation* (1905), 57.

Christian Heritage Fellowship. "The Christian Founding of Harvard." Accessed May 12, 2025. https://christianheritagefellowship.com/the-christian-founding-of-harvard/.

Christianity Today. "Jack Phillips' Masterpiece Cakeshop Wins Supreme Court Free Speech Case." June 2018. https://www.christianitytoday.com/news/2018/june/jack-phillips-masterpiece-cakeshop-wins-supreme-court-free-.html.

Cremin, Lawrence A. *American Education: The Colonial Experience, 1607–1783*. Harper & Row, 1970.

DuckDuckGo. "New England Primer." DuckDuckGo Image Search. Accessed May 27, 2025. https://duckduckgo com/?q=picture+new+england+primer&iax=images&ia=images.

Key, Francis Scott. "The Star-Spangled Banner." 1814. Verse 4. *Library of Congress*. Accessed May 28, 2025. https://www.loc.gov/item/ihas.200000017/.

Library of Congress. "Religion and the Founding of the American Republic." Accessed May 20, 2025. https://www.loc.gov/exhibits/religion/rel06.html.

Library of Congress. "Rotunda Paintings in the U.S. Capitol." https://www.aoc.gov/historic-rotunda-paintings.

Nelson, Joshua Q. "Connecticut Parents Outraged after School Shows Third Graders Video about Gender Identity without Parental Consent." *Fox News*, May 6, 2022.

Newman, Lesléa. *Heather Has Two Mommies*. 2nd ed. Somerville, MA: Candlewick Press, 2015. https://www.penguinrandomhouse.com/books/249466/heather-has-two-mommies-by-leslea-newman/9780763690427.

Newsweek*. "How the Bible Made America." December 27, 1982, 44–52.

Parks, Kristine. "Texas Professor Claims He Was Fired for Teaching X and Y Chromosomes Determine Biological Sex." *Fox News*, July 26, 2023. https://www.foxnews.com/media/texas-professor-claims-fired-teaching-x-y-chromosomes-determine-biological-sex.

Rush, Benjamin. *Letters of Benjamin Rush*, Vol. 1. Edited by L. H. Butterfield. Princeton, NJ: Princeton University Press, 1951.

Shackelford, Kelly. *First Liberty Institute Cases*. https://firstliberty.org/.

Sowell, Thomas. *Black rednecks & white liberals*. Encounter Books, 2009.

Starnes, Todd. *God Less America: Real Stories from the Front Lines of the Attack on Traditional Values*. Lake Mary, FL: FrontLine, 2014.

The Declaration of Independence. July 4, 1776. In *The American Declaration of Independence*. National Archives. https://www.archives.gov/founding-docs/declaration-transcript.

The Washington Times. "Harvard Professor: Start Treating Christians like Nazis." The Washington Times, May 10, 2016. https://www.washingtontimes.com/news/2016/may/10/harvard-professor-start-treating-christians-nazis/.

Thorpe, Francis Newton, ed. *The Federal and State Constitutions, Colonial Charters, and Other Organic Laws*. Vol. 1. Washington, DC: Government Printing Office, 1909.

U.S. Census Bureau. *Living Arrangements of Children Under 18 Years Old: 2022*. Table C3. Accessed May 28, 2025.

WallBuilders. "Franklin's Appeal for Prayer at the Constitutional Convention." Accessed May 28, 2025. https://wallbuilders.com/franklins-appeal-prayer-constitutional-convention/.

WallBuilders. "The Founding Fathers and Slavery." Accessed May 28, 2025. https://wallbuilders.com/resource/the-founding-fathers-and-slavery/.

WallBuilders. "In God We Trust." Accessed May 28, 2025. https://wallbuilders.com/in-god-we-trust/.

WallBuilders. "Unconfirmed Quotations." Accessed May 12, 2025. https://wallbuilders.com/unconfirmed-quotations/.

William J. Federer, *America's God and Country: Encyclopedia of Quotations* (Coppell, TX: FAME Publishing, 1996).

Witherspoon, "The Absolute Necessity of Salvation Through Christ," January 2, 1758, *Works*, V:278.

www.ingramcontent.com/pod-product-compliance
Lightning Source LLC
Chambersburg PA
CBHW051558120626
46551CB00013B/1575